GW01158353

Original title:
In the Shimmering Light

Author: Ophelia Ravenscroft
ISBN HARDBACK: 978-9916-88-864-3
ISBN PAPERBACK: 978-9916-88-865-0

Whispers of the Night

The stars twinkle bright,
In the blanket of the dark.
Moonlight dances softly,
As whispers ignite a spark.

Trees sway with the breeze,
Telling tales of the past.
Crickets sing their songs,
In shadows that hold fast.

A nightingale calls out,
With a melody so sweet.
The world hushes around,
As time takes a retreat.

Dreams weave through the air,
In the stillness we find peace.
Heartbeats sync with the night,
As worries gently cease.

Celestial Glitter

Stars dance in the dark sky,
Whispers of light floating by.
Galaxies spin in a cosmic ballet,
Eons in silence, night turns to day.

Comets blaze with a fiery tail,
Stories of ages in every trail.
Nebulas bloom in colors so bright,
Painting the canvas of endless night.

Spectra of Serenity

Gentle hues in the morning light,
Softly enchant the lingering night.
Nature's palette, a soothing breeze,
Calm reflections bring hearts to ease.

Mountains stand with silent grace,
Echoing peace in their steadfast place.
Rivers murmur a tranquil song,
In the quiet, where souls belong.

The Warmth of Twilight

Day's last breath, a golden glow,
Whispers of dusk start to flow.
Soft shadows weave through the glade,
As light and dark begin to fade.

Crickets sing in the cool night air,
Breezes carry sweet scents rare.
Stars awaken, timidly shine,
In twilight's embrace, all is divine.

Ethereal Gleams

Moonlight dances on silver crests,
A tranquil heart finds its rest.
Secrets woven in soft sighs,
Fleeting moments, like fireflies.

In the hush, where dreams convene,
Lies a beauty, pure and keen.
Wonders whisper through the night,
Crafting realms of sheer delight.

In the Embrace of Radiance

In dawn's gentle embrace,
The world wakes, softly shines,
Golden rays kiss the earth,
Hope dances through the pines.

Shadows retreat from light,
Whispers in the bright air,
Nature sings in colors,
Moments free from despair.

Stars fade in the morning,
Dreams melt in the sun's hue,
Each heartbeat echoes joy,
Life begins fresh and new.

Together we shall wander,
Hand in hand, light our way,
In the embrace of radiance,
We'll cherish the new day.

Light's Embrace

In the quiet of night,
A soft glow starts to rise,
Embers of the moonlight,
Casting spells in the skies.

The shadows dance around,
With a flicker and a sigh,
In light's gentle embrace,
Hearts learn how to fly.

Whispers of the starlight,
Guide our dreams to the shore,
Every glimmer a promise,
Of what we can't ignore.

Together we'll find solace,
In the warmth that we share,
In light's eternal embrace,
Our souls laid naked, bare.

Vows Beneath the Glare

In the sun's golden glare,
We stood hand in hand tight,
Promises whispered soft,
Beneath the brilliant light.

Mountains bore witness still,
As we vowed to be true,
With every heartbeat sworn,
Our spirits in loving hue.

The world around us glowed,
As the day turned to night,
Vows wrapped in the warmth,
Of love forever bright.

Together we face storms,
In the strength that you share,
Forever in my heart,
Vows made beneath the glare.

The Glowing Horizon

On the edge of the day,
Where sun meets the blue sea,
A glowing horizon waits,
For you and for me.

With each new dawn breaking,
Colors paint the sky wide,
We chase after our dreams,
With the world as our guide.

A promise in the light,
Of a future so bright,
Together, hearts ablaze,
We embrace the twilight.

As stars twinkle above,
We'll dance through the night,
On the glowing horizon,
Our love takes its flight.

A Symphony of Light

In the morning's gentle glow,
Colors burst, a radiant show.
Whispers of gold sweep through the air,
Nature sings without a care.

Dancing rays on dewdrop's face,
Each glimmer holds a warm embrace.
Melodies in every hue,
A symphony, both bright and true.

Echoes of dreams in every beam,
Lighting the world, a vibrant theme.
Together they play, day after day,
In harmony, they find their way.

The Soft Touch of Sunlight

Sunlight spills across the land,
A gentle warmth, like a soft hand.
It caresses leaves, a warm embrace,
Bringing joy to every space.

Golden rays through branches weave,
Nature smiles, it does believe.
Each beam a promise, bright and clear,
Chasing shadows, drawing near.

Moments captured in warm delight,
In the soft touch of morning light.
Life awakens, colors bloom,
Filling every heart and room.

Flickering Silhouettes

Shadows dance against the wall,
Flickering softly, they rise and fall.
A play of light in twilight's reach,
Stories told without a speech.

In the glow of the fading sun,
Each silhouette, a journey begun.
Figures merge and start to blend,
Moments lived, yet hard to mend.

Echoes of laughter, whispers of time,
In these shadows, memories rhyme.
They flicker gently, vanish fast,
Leaving traces of the past.

Daybreak's Soft Kiss

Morning breaks with gentle grace,
Daylight stretches, finds its place.
With a kiss upon the earth,
It ignites a world of birth.

Colors swirl in vibrant plays,
Blushing skies herald new days.
Nature yawns, the night retreats,
In this warmth, life gently greets.

Whispers of dawn in every breeze,
A tender touch that aims to please.
Hope arises, dreams take flight,
In daybreak's soft and golden light.

Brilliance of the Heart

In whispers soft, the heart does speak,
A glowing ember, warm and meek.
Each beat a note, a sacred art,
Illuminating love's bright start.

A tapestry of dreams unfolds,
With threads of joy that life upholds.
In every glance, a story was spun,
Two souls unite, their journey begun.

Through trials faced and battles won,
In stillness found, the way is run.
Together they rise, never apart,
Forever shines the brilliance of the heart.

A treasure rare, this bond so true,
In every heartbeat, I find you.
Like stars at night, we find our way,
In love's embrace, we choose to stay.

The Dance of Reflections

In mirrors cast, our shadows play,
Each turn a lesson, night and day.
With graceful steps, the light we find,
In echoes soft, our hearts aligned.

The world a stage where dreams collide,
In silver glow, our worries slide.
Together we weave, a tale so bright,
In the dance of reflections, hearts take flight.

We spin through moments, both dark and light,
In silent whispers, our souls ignite.
Every glance holds eternity's chance,
As we sway to the rhythm of chance.

In the stillness, our spirits soar,
A symphony crafted, forever more.
With each reflection, we learn to see,
The beauty in you, the beauty in me.

A Symphony of Light

In dawn's embrace, the day begins,
A choir of colors, where hope wins.
Each ray a note, harmonious and bright,
Composing a symphony of light.

As shadows fade and spirits rise,
We sing our truths, beneath vast skies.
In every heartbeat, a sound so clear,
Melodies echo, drawing us near.

Together we stand, a vibrant sound,
In the harmonies of life, we are found.
With love's refrain, we tread the night,
Creating a world, bathed in pure light.

So let us dance in this radiant glow,
Where passion ignites and dreams can flow.
In every moment, a song takes flight,
An endless journey, a symphony of light.

Aurora's Kiss

As dawn unfolds, the canvas glows,
In hues of pink, the world bestows.
A gentle brush, a tender bliss,
Awakening all with Aurora's kiss.

The morning dew, a crystal sight,
Reflects the promise of hope and light.
Each petal's whisper, a soft embrace,
In nature's arms, we find our place.

With every breeze, the dreams take flight,
The horizon calls, a beacon bright.
Together we trace the sky's vast span,
In Aurora's glow, we walk hand in hand.

So let us cherish this fleeting hour,
Embracing magic in every flower.
With hearts alight and spirits free,
In the kiss of dawn, we find our key.

Heaven's Playground

Soft whispers of the breeze
Carrying laughter high
Where clouds play hide and seek
Underneath the endless sky.

Children of the stars
Dreaming in the light
Wildflowers dance around
In colors pure and bright.

Sunbeams weave a tapestry
Of gold upon the ground
While shadows kiss the valley
In a quiet, sacred sound.

Moments drift like petals
On a gentle stream
In heaven's playground, joy resides
Embraced within a dream.

The Dance of Light and Shadow

In the fading twilight glow,
Shadows stretch and bend,
While whispers of the evening,
Invite the night to mend.

A flicker here, a shimmer there,
As moonlight starts to play,
The dance of dark and light unfolds,
In a mystical ballet.

Stars twirl in the heavens,
As echoes softly sigh,
Painting dreams with subtle hues,
In the canvas of the sky.

With every twinkle, every gleam,
A story feels alive,
The night weaves tales of wonder,
As shadows come to thrive.

Illuminated Dreams

A lantern in the dark,
Shining bright and clear,
Guiding all the lost souls,
Drawing them near.

Across the glimmering seas,
Where wishes take their flight,
Lies a realm of dreams aglow,
Bathed in soft twilight.

Each spark a tiny story,
Whispered on the breeze,
Inviting hearts to wander,
And find their inner peace.

In the illuminated night,
Hope dances on the streams,
As the world embraces light,
Awakening the dreams.

Chasing Glimmers

Glimmers in the distance,
Calling out my name,
I chase the fleeting whispers,
On the edge of flame.

Through fields of wild daisies,
And rivers shining bright,
I wander in the twilight,
Seeking glimpses of the light.

Every step a heartbeat,
Every sigh a chance,
To catch a glimpse of magic,
In the evening's dance.

Chasing glimmers, I embrace,
The journey yet undone,
For every spark I follow,
Leads me closer to the sun.

Journey Through the Glow

In the hush of twilight's embrace,
Dreams begin to softly trace.
Each star a whisper, a tale untold,
Guiding hearts through paths of gold.

Beneath the sky, the echoes play,
Every step, a new array.
With shadows dancing, faint and light,
We wander deep into the night.

A glimmer here, a shimmer there,
The essence of hope fills the air.
In the calm, we find our way,
Onward through the fading day.

With every breath, the world unfolds,
A tapestry of dreams, so bold.
In this journey, hearts will grow,
Together through the vibrant glow.

Shimmers of Yesterday

In the quiet of the past,
Memories linger, shadows cast.
Each laugh a thread, each tear a hue,
Woven in time, both old and new.

The sun sets low, as stories fade,
Yet echoes of love will never jade.
Fleeting moments, soft and bright,
Dance like fireflies in the night.

Whispers of time, so bittersweet,
In the heart, they find their beat.
Through the corridors of the mind,
Shimmers of yesterday, entwined.

With every glance, a spark ignites,
Bringing warmth to chilly nights.
In the stillness, we hold tight,
To shimmers of dreams that take flight.

Touched by the Aurora

Beneath the northern skies we stand,
Colors dance, both wild and grand.
A ballet of lights that weave and flow,
Touched by the magic of the aurora's glow.

In the silent whispers of the night,
Nature reveals her wondrous sight.
Each wave, a thrill, each pulse, a sigh,
As the heavens paint a lullaby.

With fingers outstretched, we reach above,
Chasing the echoes of our love.
In the brilliance, we find our place,
Wrapped in the warmth of this embrace.

Awash in hues of green and blue,
The cosmos sings, as dreams come true.
Touched by wonder, hand in hand,
Together beneath this mystical land.

The Glow of Memories

In the attic of thoughts, dust motes swirl,
Bringing back days, where time would twirl.
Each picture frames a fleeting glance,
The glow of memories in a dance.

Whispers of laughter, echoes of youth,
Moments collected, fragments of truth.
The heart recalls, with joy and pain,
The magic of when we were unchained.

Through the years, like flickering light,
Guiding us through the darkest night.
Each heartbeat pulses with the past,
The glow of memories held steadfast.

In every corner, a story waits,
Unlocking love, as the soul creates.
As time flows on, we hold them near,
The glow of memories, forever clear.

Beneath the Sparkling Veil

Underneath the stars so bright,
Whispers dance in the night air.
Dreams take flight on wings of light,
In silence, secrets we share.

The moon casts a silver gleam,
Painting shadows on the ground.
Together in this fleeting dream,
We lose ourselves, love unbound.

Each flicker tells a story old,
Of moments captured like dew.
Beneath the veil, we find gold,
In every glance, forever new.

The Glow of Timeless Moments

In the warmth of gentle days,
Memories weave through every smile.
Time stands still in golden rays,
A heartbeat felt across each mile.

The laughter echoes soft and clear,
Boundless joy in every glance.
With every moment, we draw near,
In timeless love, we dare to dance.

Our hands entwined, we boldly go,
Chasing dreams with hearts aflame.
In this glow, we learn to grow,
In the beauty of love's name.

Chasing Sunbeams

Through fields of gold the children run,
With laughter ringing in the air.
Each sunbeam kissed by morning sun,
A fleeting moment, bright and rare.

They chase the light with joyful glee,
As shadows dance upon the ground.
In innocence, they wander free,
Where every heartbeat knows no bound.

And every ray, a promise made,
Of adventures yet to unfold.
In the glow, hopes never fade,
As dreams of childhood painted gold.

Revelations in Glinting Shadows

In the quiet where whispers dwell,
Secrets glint like gems unseen.
Layers peel, casting a spell,
Revealing truths that lie between.

The sun dips low, shadows will creep,
Fleeting glimpses of hidden grace.
In the twilight, mysteries seep,
In shadows, we find our place.

Each flicker holds a tale untold,
Of hopes that shimmer in the night.
Revelations, daring and bold,
Awaken dreams with gentle light.

Glimmering Whispers

In the quiet night, stars gleam bright,
Softly whispering tales of light.
Gentle breezes carry dreams,
Wrapped in silver, or so it seems.

Moonbeams dance on leaves so fair,
Breathing secrets through the air.
Each glimmer speaks of hopes untold,
In this tapestry of night, we behold.

Flickering shadows play on walls,
Echoing laughter, as twilight calls.
The world is hushed, but hearts ignite,
With glimmering whispers of the night.

Embrace the magic, let it flow,
As stars above begin to glow.
In these moments, we find our peace,
With glimmering whispers, joys increase.

Brightening Shadows

As dawn breaks with a soft embrace,
Shadows recoil in morning's grace.
Colors burst, a canvas new,
Painting dreams in vibrant hue.

Golden rays reach for the ground,
In every corner, life is found.
Whispers of light, they softly spread,
Chasing the night and fears we dread.

Flower petals stretch and yawn,
Greeting the beauty of a new dawn.
With every heartbeat, hope will rise,
Brightening shadows, the world complies.

In the embrace of day's warm kiss,
Every moment feels like bliss.
Together we'll dance, hand in hand,
In the brightening shadows, we will stand.

The Dazzle of Dusk

When the sun dips low, hues entwine,
Crimson and gold, a feast divine.
Clouds painted soft in shades of fire,
Whispers of night, our hearts inspire.

As silence drapes the fading light,
The world prepares for the starry night.
Flickers of dusk in the cooling air,
Enveloping dreams with tender care.

Cicadas hum their evening song,
As shadows stretch, the night grows strong.
The dazzle of dusk, a fleeting show,
In every moment, we let love grow.

Beneath the sky's enchanting veil,
We find our stories, love will prevail.
In the dazzle of dusk, we find our way,
Embracing the night, come what may.

Moonlit Murmurs

Underneath the silver glow,
Lies a world we long to know.
Moonlit whispers roam so free,
Telling tales of mystery.

Softly treading on the ground,
Echoes of secrets all around.
In the night, our spirits soar,
In moonlit murmurs, we explore.

Stars like diamonds grace the sky,
In this moment, we won't shy.
With every heartbeat, magic grows,
In moonlit murmur, the soul knows.

As we wander through the night,
We'll embrace the gentle light.
With whispered dreams beneath the moon,
In moonlit murmurs, hearts attune.

Glistening Horizons

The sun dips low, a fiery glow,
Painting skies in crimson hues.
Waves dance lightly on the shore,
Whispers of the evening muse.

Seagulls glide on fleeting breeze,
Their calls a song to close the day.
With shadows stretching, dreams take flight,
In twilight's grasp, we drift away.

Stars begin to peep at night,
A canvas brushed in silver light.
Each twinkle tells a tale of old,
Of journeys walked and dreams retold.

The horizon glimmers with soft hope,
As night unfolds its velvet cloak.
In every shimmer, a promise shines,
A world awake where wonder binds.

Threads of Illumination

In the tapestry of night, stars loom,
Each one a thread spun bright and fine.
They weave stories of distant worlds,
In shadows cast, they brightly shine.

The moon, a lantern in the dark,
Guides wandering souls on their way.
With silver beams that dance and play,
Revealing paths where heartstrings sway.

Amongst the darkness, hope stirs bright,
Sparks of joy within the gloom.
Each thread connects us, near and far,
In this vast web, dreams find room.

Let the threads of light unite,
In every heart, a flame ignites.
Together we'll weave our tales anew,
In this tapestry, life's vibrant view.

The Sparkling Canvas

Brush strokes of dawn paint the sky,
With hues of gold and soft pastel.
Each morning brings a chance to dream,
In every drop, a story to tell.

Clouds drift softly like whispers, light,
As artists blend the day with grace.
Every moment, a stroke of time,
On this vast canvas, we find our place.

The river reflects the morning glow,
A shimmering path, so bright and free.
With waves like laughter, they call us near,
In nature's chorus, we find harmony.

Let us create in vibrant shades,
Each heartbeat echoes in the scene.
In every glance, there lies a spark,
On this canvas, love intervenes.

Where Daybreak Glows

Awake, the world begins to stir,
As shadows fade in morning light.
A gentle breeze whispers softly,
Inviting warmth to banish night.

Birds begin their morning song,
Each note a promise of the day.
Flowers open to greet the sun,
In radiant colors, they sway.

The horizon blushes, painted bright,
With shades of orange, pink, and blue.
A tapestry of time unwinds,
In every beam, a dream anew.

Here where daybreak finds its grace,
We gather strength to face the day.
With every dawn, the world ignites,
In this dance of light, we'll stay.

Whispers of Radiance

In the quiet night, stars hum,
A soft glow speaks, the world is numb.
Moonlit dreams weave through the trees,
Whispers of light, dancing in the breeze.

Shadows stretch, embracing the dark,
Every glimmer holds a hidden spark.
Gentle secrets float on the air,
A symphony of silence, tender and rare.

Time slows down, the heart takes flight,
In the tender hush, the soul ignites.
Radiance weaves through time's embrace,
Reminding us of love's warm trace.

In every corner, the light shall creep,
Awakening visions from our sleep.
Whispers of radiance softly call,
In the night, we find our all.

Echoes of the Sun

Golden rays spill, a radiant tide,
Kissing the earth, where dreams abide.
Echoes of warmth, in every beam,
The sun's gentle laughter, a waking dream.

Buds unfurl, under celestial gaze,
Nature sways in joyful praise.
The sky ignites with colors anew,
A canvas painted in bright, bold hue.

Bright melodies dance on a breeze,
Songs of warmth, that never cease.
Every moment, a promise spun,
In the heart's depths, the echoes run.

As day melts into twilight's hand,
The sun whispers softly, its final stand.
Echoes linger, throughout the night,
Filling our souls with tender light.

Twilight's Embrace

When the day bids its soft farewell,
Twilight cloaks the world in its spell.
Colors blend in a silent sigh,
As the stars awaken in the sky.

Shadows bloom in the fading light,
Crickets serenade the coming night.
Soft whispers trace the evening air,
Promises whispered, hearts laid bare.

In twilight's arms, the world stands still,
A moment captured, a heart to fill.
Glimmers of hope in the dusk's sweet glow,
Guiding us gently to where love flows.

As darkness deepens, dreams take flight,
In twilight's embrace, everything feels right.
A soft lullaby of light and grace,
Revealing life's beauty in vast space.

A Luminous Journey

Footsteps echo on paths of dreams,
Each turn adorned with radiant beams.
Whispers of hope in the morning dew,
A luminous journey begins anew.

Through forests deep and mountains high,
We chase the light in an endless sky.
With every heartbeat, a story told,
A tapestry woven in threads of gold.

Stars guide us through the darkest night,
Illuminating our way with bright light.
As we wander through time's gentle flow,
The luminous journey teaches us to grow.

In every moment, a spark to ignite,
In the dance of life, we find our height.
Hand in hand, we'll venture on,
Through the luminous journey, never alone.

Luminescent Dreams

In the quiet night, stars unfold,
Whispers of tales untold.
Softly they dance in silvery beams,
Guiding us through luminescent dreams.

The moon's gentle glow begins to rise,
Painting the world with tranquil sighs.
Hopes take flight on wings of light,
Illuminating shadows, banishing night.

Wanderers roam in silvery tides,
Searching for solace where magic abides.
With every thought, the night ignites,
Crafting a canvas where fantasy writes.

Awake in the shimmer, let worries cease,
Wrap yourself in the warmth of peace.
For in these dreams, forever we'll soar,
Chasing the light, forevermore.

Beneath the Aurora

Veils of color, dancing above,
Nature's canvas, a work of love.
Swirling greens with purple threads,
Beneath the aurora, our spirits spread.

Whispers of night call out to me,
In this wonder, we're wild and free.
Captured in time, a fleeting glance,
Beneath the lights, we find our dance.

Stars shimmer softly, shadows take flight,
Bathed in the magic, we chase the night.
Every brushstroke a moment divine,
Beneath the aurora, our souls intertwine.

Let us wander under spectral skies,
Breathing in dreams, where beauty lies.
Together we'll stroll, hand in hand,
Beneath the aurora, in this enchanted land.

Dappled Sunlight

Golden rays break through the leaves,
Painting the world as nature weaves.
Dappled patterns dance on the ground,
In the gentle whisper, beauty's found.

Meadows awaken with colors bright,
Flowers blooming in morning light.
Breezes carry fragrance sweet,
In dappled sunlight, hearts skip a beat.

Wandering paths where shadows play,
Moments unfold in a joyous ballet.
Each flicker a promise, a secret share,
In sunlight's embrace, we breathe the air.

Golden hours drift into dusk,
Leaving behind a gentle husk.
But memories linger when day has gone,
In dappled sunlight, our spirits drawn.

Shimmering Secrets

In the depths of night, secrets hide,
Whispers of magic, a haunting guide.
Stars mirror dreams in an endless sea,
Shimmering secrets, just you and me.

Every glance holds a spark of fate,
In the silence, we contemplate.
Unraveling tales in the silver shade,
Shimmering secrets, our fears allayed.

Moments woven with delicate threads,
Each heartbeat a promise the universe spreads.
In the twilight glow, we find our way,
Shimmering secrets, in love we stay.

Embrace the night, let your heart soar,
For in the shadows, we'll always explore.
Together we'll cherish the things we share,
Shimmering secrets, a bond so rare.

Threads of Radiant Dreams

In twilight's whisper, shadows gleam,
Woven together, we chase a dream.
Stars twinkle softly, secrets unfold,
Threads of hope in silver and gold.

Each moment captured, a fleeting glance,
In the fabric of night, we dare to dance.
With every heartbeat, we rise and dive,
Threads of our dreams, where we feel alive.

Gentle horizons greet the dawn,
Carrying whispers of dreams reborn.
Together we wander, hand in hand,
In the tapestry of this enchanted land.

Fleeting like fireflies, our wishes soar,
Threads of radiant dreams forevermore.

Portraits in Light

Amidst the glow, a canvas spreads,
Each stroke a memory, each hue it sheds.
Capturing laughter, the joy we share,
Portraits in light, a world laid bare.

In shadows and colors, we find our way,
Moments like brushstrokes in bright array.
With whispers of magic, the heart ignites,
Creating a gallery of shimmering sights.

Every heartbeat echoes in vibrant hues,
A masterpiece formed from the love we choose.
Layers of dreams in magnificent flight,
Crafting a tale in portraits of light.

As the day fades, our story will gleam,
In portraits of light, we're living the dream.

Dancing Reflections

On the surface of water, the moonlight plays,
Dancing reflections in delicate ways.
Each ripple whispers a tale of delight,
Under the stars in the depth of night.

Soft as the breeze, our shadows entwine,
In the twilight's embrace, our hearts align.
With every turn, the world spins around,
In dancing reflections, our joy is found.

The rhythm of nature, the pulse of the day,
Guides us through moments that drift away.
Together we twirl, in love's gentle trance,
In the dance of reflections, we take our chance.

And when the dawn breaks, our spirits will shine,
In the dancing reflections, your heart will be mine.

Glimmers of Dawn

As the night surrenders to morning's embrace,
Glimmers of dawn paint the sky's face.
With whispers of light, the shadows retreat,
Awakening dreams as the day finds its beat.

In soft hues of orange, pink, and gold,
The stories of night become tales to be told.
Each ray a promise, a new chance to start,
Glimmers of dawn tugging at every heart.

Nature awakens, the world stirs alive,
In the glow of the morn, we learn to thrive.
With each fleeting moment, the past bids adieu,
In glimmers of dawn, we find hope anew.

So as light breaks through, let your spirit ascend,
Chasing glimmers of dawn, on this we depend.

Shards of Brilliance

In silence they shimmer, secrets unfold,
Glimmers of truth in colors so bold.
Each piece tells a tale, a moment caught,
In shards of brilliance, wisdom is sought.

Fragments of dreams dance in the light,
Casting reflections, a beautiful sight.
With every glance, a story to share,
Shards of brilliance, floating in air.

The heart feels the pull, drawn by the glow,
Each shard a reminder of what we know.
Together they form a mosaic divine,
In the dance of colors, our spirits entwine.

So gather these shards, let them collide,
In the chaos of beauty, in brilliance, we glide.
A canvas of moments, forever they gleam,
In life's rich tapestry, we weave our dream.

A Tapestry of Glow

Threads of light weave a tapestry bright,
Colors of day fade into night.
Each layer a whisper, soft and clear,
A tapestry of glow, drawing us near.

Silken strands of laughter, shimmering bold,
Stories of warmth in the fibers of gold.
Kaleidoscope visions, intertwined fate,
In this vivid fabric, we celebrate.

The patterns of love in a delicate twist,
Moments together, in joy we persist.
Every stitch a heartbeat, close up or far,
In a tapestry of glow, we find who we are.

So let us embrace this radiant weave,
In the warmth of our hearts, we dare to believe.
In the light of togetherness, we come alive,
A tapestry of glow, where dreams thrive.

The Radiant Veil

A veil of brilliance drapes the night,
Whispers of starlight, a soft, gentle sight.
Each fold a mystery, secrets concealed,
In the radiant veil, dreams are revealed.

The moon casts shadows, dancing so free,
Embraced in the glow of what we can't see.
With every heartbeat, the world turns still,
Under the secret of the radiant veil.

Hope woven softly in silver and blue,
Glimmers of magic in drops of dew.
The night holds its breath, waiting for dawn,
In the folds of the veil, dreams carry on.

So wander beneath this luminous guise,
With wonder-filled hearts and open eyes.
For in the embrace of the starlit reveal,
We find our place under the radiant veil.

Beyond the Golden Haze

Golden hues shimmer in the soft morning light,
Promises linger, igniting the night.
Beyond the haze, where the shadows play,
We search for the dawn, a brand new day.

Steps through the mist, where silence resides,
Carried by whispers, on gentle tides.
In the warmth of hope, we rise and fall,
Beyond the golden haze, we answer the call.

A journey unwritten, the path unfolds,
Stories of wonder, in echoes retold.
With every heartbeat, the adventure clears,
Beyond the golden haze, we face our fears.

So dance through the dawn, feel life's embrace,
In the glow of the morning, we find our place.
Forever we're woven in the warmth of the rays,
As we venture onward, beyond the golden haze.

In the Wake of Dawn

The sun peeks over the hill,
Soft whispers in the air,
Morning dew on blades chill,
Nature wakes from its lair.

Birds sing a sweet refrain,
Colors burst into the light,
A world washed free of rain,
Preparing for new delight.

Trees stretch their arms wide,
Nurtured by the golden glow,
A quiet river's glide,
Reflects the day's warm flow.

Hope dances in the sky,
Promises begin anew,
In this moment we fly,
As daylight breaks on cue.

Glinting Silhouettes

Shadows flicker on the wall,
Mysterious figures loom,
Underneath the moon's soft call,
A dance plays in the gloom.

Branches sway with secret grace,
Beneath the starry veil,
In this enigmatic space,
Dreams linger, vast and pale.

Soft laughter in the night,
As echoes twist and bend,
Glinting shades in silver light,
Where stories never end.

Quiet whispers find their time,
Ghostly tales take their flight,
In twilight's gentle rhyme,
We lose ourselves in the night.

The Luster of Existence

Life sparkles with each breath,
In the moments we reclaim,
From the cradle unto death,
Each heartbeat, a flickering flame.

Time holds its golden thread,
Stitching memories in place,
With every word that's said,
We carve our own embrace.

Wonders bloom in the mundane,
In simple joys we find,
A universe in our veins,
Connected, heart and mind.

We dance through the years we roam,
Chasing dreams, tender and bold,
In the luster, we call home,
Life's tapestry unfolds.

Rays of Enchantment

Golden streaks paint the sky,
Awakening the earth below,
As day begins to sigh,
In the sun's warm, gentle glow.

Fields shimmer with delight,
Touched by morning's embrace,
With petals shining bright,
Nature's soft, enchanting grace.

The world spins in slow dance,
Wrapped in a tender spell,
Each glance a fleeting chance,
In magic where we dwell.

The heart feels every ray,
As dreams take their own flight,
In this beautiful display,
We bask in pure delight.

Radiant Reflections

In the mirror of the dawn,
Shadows dance on the lake,
Whispers of light softly speak,
A new day's promise to make.

Golden hues paint the skies,
Fleeting moments take flight,
Each reflection holds a truth,
Radiant dreams in the light.

Ripples play on the water,
Timeless tales they weave,
Every glance sparks a memory,
In the heart, they believe.

Nature's canvas shines bright,
Mirroring hopes from above,
In this tranquil solitude,
We find the essence of love.

Luminescent Journeys

Footprints trace paths unknown,
Across the twilight gleam,
Each step a story unfolds,
Woven into a dream.

Starlight guides the wanderer,
Through valleys deep and wide,
Luminescent trails beckon,
With the moon as a guide.

Every heartbeat's a compass,
Drawing maps of the soul,
Illuminated by passion,
In pursuit of the whole.

Onward to horizons vast,
Where the light dares to play,
Journeying through the darkness,
Finding joy in the sway.

Cosmic Dust and Glorious Rays

In the cradle of the night,
Stars like jewels shine bright,
Cosmic dust in the velvet,
Guiding hearts toward light.

Galaxies whisper dreams,
In the silence they bloom,
Glorious rays from afar,
Chasing away the gloom.

A tapestry of wonder,
Weaving tales of the past,
In the firmament's embrace,
Moments eternal, vast.

Hearts collide in stardust,
Eclipsing the mundane,
Underneath celestial smiles,
Love is never in vain.

Shimmering Whispers

Beneath the willow's grace,
Gentle breezes entwine,
Shimmering whispers at dusk,
Softly through branches align.

Every leaf tells a story,
Of the sun and of rain,
A symphony of silence,
Where the heart can remain.

Moonlight drapes like a veil,
Over dreams yet to seek,
Shimmering whispers linger,
In the night, they speak.

Embracing night's caress,
With echoes that flow,
In the garden of wonders,
Magic continues to grow.

Uplifted by Radiance

Golden beams descend with grace,
Awakening the sleeping place.
Hearts embrace the warming glow,
Nature whispers soft and low.

Skyward, dreams begin to soar,
Wings unfurl, we seek for more.
Radiance fuels our hopeful spark,
Guiding us from light to dark.

Each ray, a promise yet untold,
Stories of the brave and bold.
Hand in hand, we stand so bright,
Together, we ignite the light.

With each dawn, new paths we find,
Radiant love, forever entwined.
Embracing all, both near and far,
In the light, we are who we are.

Flickering Tales

In shadows where the whispers dwell,
Flickering flames begin to tell.
Tales of love and loss reborn,
Of silent nights and hopes adorned.

Each spark ignites a memory,
An echo of what's meant to be.
Through tales both bright and bittersweet,
We gather 'round, our hearts repeat.

Voices dance upon the air,
Sharing secrets, souls laid bare.
In the glow, we find our place,
Wrapped in warmth, and held in grace.

Flickering tales will never fade,
In the heart, a shining cascade.
So let us linger in this light,
In every spark, a soul ignites.

The Luminous Horizon

Beyond the mountains, light unfolds,
A canvas painted in vibrant golds.
Whispers of a brand-new day,
Chasing shadows far away.

The horizon beckons us with grace,
A journey starts, a sacred space.
Step by step, we navigate,
Toward the gleam, we elevate.

In the glow, our spirits rise,
Reflections drawn in azure skies.
Every dream, a thread we weave,
In this magic, we believe.

So let the dawn embrace our soul,
In the luminous, we feel whole.
Together, hand in hand we strive,
On this horizon, we arrive.

Laughter in Light

Beneath the sun, laughter plays,
Echoing through radiant days.
Each giggle sparkles in the air,
Joy unfolds, beyond compare.

Children's voices, pure and bright,
Dance like fireflies in the night.
With every chuckle, shadows flee,
In laughter, we find unity.

Moments shared beneath the trees,
Whispers carried by the breeze.
In the light, our spirits sing,
Celebrating what joy can bring.

So take a breath, let worries fade,
In this laughter, love is laid.
Together, let our hearts take flight,
Forever basking in the light.

Glimmers of Dawn

In the hush of morning light,
Soft colors break the night.
A gentle breeze begins to sway,
Welcoming the brand new day.

Mountains bathed in radiant glow,
As the rivers start to flow.
Birds arise with joyful song,
In the dawn where dreams belong.

Petals lift in silent praise,
Kissed by sun's embracing rays.
Nature wakes with vibrant hue,
Painting skies in every view.

Time stands still, the world holds its breath,
In the beauty born from death.
Each moment, a fleeting chance,
In the light of dawn's sweet dance.

Dancing with Radiance

Underneath a sapphire sky,
Where the softest breezes sigh.
Fields of gold stretch far and wide,
As the sun begins to glide.

Cascades of light twirl and spin,
In the warmth where dreams begin.
Every leaf takes on a glow,
In this dance, we lose our woe.

Silken shadows play their part,
Bringing joy to every heart.
With each breath, the world ignites,
In a tapestry of lights.

Hold my hand, let shadows flee,
In this radiant harmony.
Together we will paint the skies,
With the magic in our eyes.

Whispers of the First Ray

Quiet moments hold the sun,
As the day has just begun.
Whispers float upon the breeze,
Carried softly through the trees.

Gold embraces every leaf,
In the dawn, devoid of grief.
Nature's lullaby unfolds,
As the warmth begins to hold.

Every shadow starts to fade,
In the light that hope has made.
Promises of joy and cheer,
In the first ray, calling near.

With each breath, the world awakes,
In the stillness, love it makes.
Morning's kiss, a tender plea,
Unfolds life in harmony.

A Caress of Golden Hues

Brush of light upon the land,
Caressing all, it takes its stand.
A dance of colors, bright and bold,
In the stories yet untold.

Saffron streaks across the skies,
Painting dreams where beauty lies.
Each moment, a gift divine,
In the heart, its warmth we find.

Gazing out where horizons meet,
Every heartbeat keeps the beat.
In this canvas, life takes flight,
Bearing whispers of pure light.

Hold close this tender time we share,
In the glow, we find our care.
A caress from golden hues,
In this dance, we will not lose.

Beyond the Breaking Day

The dawn unfolds its gentle grace,
A canvas painted in soft hues.
Whispers of night begin to fade,
As light awakens hidden views.

Golden rays embrace the land,
Awakening life from its slumber.
Nature stirs with a soft command,
Each moment rich, a soft wonder.

In the air, the promise sings,
Of hope and dreams that soar on high.
A new beginning softly clings,
As shadows bow to morning sky.

With every breath, a chance to grow,
Beyond the breaking of the day.
A world renewed, a sacred flow,
Awaits in shimmering arrays.

Luminous Sojourns

We wander paths of starlit dust,
Through gentle nights, on whispered trails.
With every step, our hearts entrust,
The universe within us sails.

The moon, a beacon high above,
Illuminates the dreams we chase.
In silent awe, we share our love,
Each moment etched, a fleeting grace.

With every glance, the world unfolds,
A tapestry of light and shade.
In luminous sojourns, we behold,
The beauty in the journeys made.

We dance beneath the cosmic tide,
With twinkling stars to guide our way.
Together on this wondrous ride,
We seek the dawn beyond the gray.

When Radiance Awakens

When radiance awakens the morn,
A symphony of colors play.
The air aglow with dreams reborn,
And shadows drift, far swept away.

The earth embraces tender light,
Each flower sways in sweet delight.
As sunbeams spill through leaves so bright,
The world transforms, a pure invite.

With laughter dancing on the breeze,
We celebrate the day's embrace.
In every glance, our spirits seize,
A chance to bask in nature's grace.

When radiance awakens our souls,
We find our place, we claim our song.
Together, we will fill the roles,
Of life and love, where we belong.

Echoes of the Gleaming Horizon

In twilight's glow, the echoes call,
Where dreams and daylight intertwine.
The gleaming horizon meets us all,
In whispers soft, our fates align.

The stars ignite, a cosmic dance,
With stories spun from worlds afar.
In every pulse, a fleeting chance,
To chase the dawn, to find our star.

We stand as one on this vast stage,
With hearts ablaze, our spirits free.
In every whisper, every page,
The echoes sing our tapestry.

So let us wander, hand in hand,
Through realms where night and day conspire.
In echoes sweet, we take our stand,
Embracing dreams that lift us higher.

The Glow Within

In the silence of the night,
A whisper stirs the soul,
Embers of the heart ignite,
A warmth that makes us whole.

Flickers dance against the dark,
A beacon calling near,
In every shadow, there's a spark,
Illuminating fear.

The glow within will always rise,
No matter what we face,
A guiding light, a sweet surprise,
In life's most tender place.

Together we will shine so bright,
With love to light the way,
In darkness, we will find our sight,
And turn the night to day.

Shadows Brilliantly Cast

Underneath the moonlit sky,
Our silhouettes entwine,
Shadows whisper soft goodbyes,
Yet hold a love divine.

In every curve, a story flows,
Captured in the night,
Moments shared, as twilight glows,
Transforming dark to light.

With each step, the shadows sway,
In dance, they weave their art,
Brilliant echoes of the day,
Reflecting every heart.

As dawn breaks through, they gently fade,
But memories will last,
In every smile, a sense portrayed,
Of shadows brilliantly cast.

Light's Tender Caress

Morning breaks with soft embrace,
A touch of purest gold,
Light's tender caress on my face,
Brings warmth against the cold.

Every ray a gentle kiss,
On petals fresh with dew,
In nature's song, we find our bliss,
As colors come to view.

In the quiet, whispers play,
Among the leaves so green,
Light guides us on our way,
To places yet unseen.

So let us bask in this delight,
In every sunlit phase,
For in this world, the purest light,
Is love's enduring blaze.

Radiant Pathways

Winding paths of golden rays,
Invite us to explore,
Through twisting trails of summer days,
And memories we store.

Each step taken, hearts will soar,
With visions clear and bright,
The radiant pathways we adore,
Lead us into the light.

In gardens where the wildflowers bloom,
We breathe in every sight,
In nature's space, we find our room,
Our spirits take to flight.

So hand in hand, we'll walk this way,
With laughter as our guide,
For on this radiant pathway,
Love will be our stride.

Flickers of Hope

In the dark, a whisper sings,
A promise wrapped in fragile wings.
Through shadows deep, a light appears,
It chases away the weight of fears.

With every dawn, the sun will rise,
Painting gold across the skies.
Let dreams ignite in hearts anew,
Flickers of hope that guide us through.

In the quiet moments, softly tread,
Where hopes are born and fear is shed.
Embrace the spark, let courage flow,
For hidden light will surely grow.

Beneath the weight, the spirit soars,
Breaking chains, unlocking doors.
With every step, we find our way,
Flickers of hope, here to stay.

Starlit Pathways

Beneath the canvas of the night,
Stars like jewels, a wondrous sight.
Each twinkle speaks of journeys far,
Guiding us with the light of a star.

In the hush of twilight's embrace,
We find our dreams, our sacred space.
With every step on this starlit trail,
Hearts entwined, we cannot fail.

The whispers of the cosmos call,
In harmony, we stand tall.
Hand in hand, we walk as one,
Under the gaze of ancient suns.

The paths we tread are painted bright,
With every star, we claim our light.
Together we'll dance, forever free,
On starlit pathways, you and me.

Elysian Gleam

In a meadow where dreams converge,
Soft whispers of the winds emerge.
Golden rays through branches weave,
An elysian gleam, we believe.

With every flower blooming wide,
Painted hues, nature's pride.
In the stillness, time stands still,
Embraced by magic, hearts do fill.

The gentle brook sings a lullaby,
Crickets chirp as night draws nigh.
In this realm where spirits play,
Elysian gleam leads the way.

Beneath the stars, we find our peace,
In the beauty, our worries cease.
Together we share this tranquil scene,
In the glow of Elysian sheen.

The Softest Glow

In the hush of the evening air,
A gentle light, a moment rare.
Soft shadows dance upon the ground,
The softest glow of love is found.

With every heartbeat, warmth ignites,
Filling the world with tender sights.
A whisper shared, a hand held tight,
Guiding us through the calm of night.

Embers flicker, dreams take flight,
In the dark, we are the light.
With eyes aglow, paths intertwine,
Finding solace, hearts align.

In this moment, time is slow,
Together we bask in the softest glow.
Forever cherished, side by side,
In love's embrace, we will abide.

A Tapestry of Glowing Dreams

Threads of silver weave through night,
Glowing softly, a gentle light.
Whispers of wishes softly hum,
In the fabric, stories come.

Stars gently twinkle, secrets shared,
In this place, no hearts impaired.
Colors blend in a vibrant dance,
Embracing all in a trance.

Carried forth on a velvet breeze,
Each moment captured, time agrees.
Dancing shadows, cosmic seam,
Creating beauty in a dream.

With every stitch, the world unfolds,
A tapestry of dreams retold.
In the quiet, we find our way,
Guided by the night to day.

Twilight's Embrace

The sun dips low, a fiery glow,
Painting skies in undertones slow.
Whispers of dusk lace the night,
Cradling stars in fading light.

Deep shadows stretch, the day departs,
Twilight whispers to weary hearts.
A gentle sigh, the world takes pause,
In this magic, there's no cause.

Cool winds murmur, a soft caress,
Nature's beauty, a sweet finesse.
Every heartbeat, a part of grace,
Captured in twilight's warm embrace.

As darkness falls, dreams take flight,
Guided by the moon's pure white.
In the silence, hopes ignite,
Awaiting dawn, a new daylight.

Flickers of Hope

In the shadows, a spark does glow,
Flickers of dreams continually flow.
Holding tight to the light we see,
Hope ignites in you and me.

Moments fleeting, so fragile, bright,
Whispers of strength in the night.
With each flicker, a journey starts,
Lighting paths within our hearts.

The dawn will break, the darkness fade,
In the quiet, the fears dismayed.
Breathe in deep, let the light bloom,
Casting aside the weight of gloom.

Together we rise, hand in hand,
United strong, together we stand.
Flickers grow into flames that soar,
Hope's gentle whispers, forevermore.

The Prism of Serenity

Colors dance in peaceful streams,
Reflecting thoughts, cradling dreams.
A prism shines, a gentle light,
Washing worries, pure and bright.

In still waters, the heart finds peace,
Moments linger, tension cease.
Nature's hue, in vibrant sway,
Guides the soul at end of day.

Breathe deeply in this sacred place,
Feel the grace, the soft embrace.
Each colorful ray, a soothing balm,
Serenity wraps with tranquil calm.

As day turns night, a soft refrain,
Echoes softly, joy and pain.
In the prism's glow, we find our way,
Serenity's gift at close of day.

Illuminated Paths

Through winding trails of light we tread,
Each step a story, whispers spread.
Beneath the stars, our dreams take flight,
In every shadow, there's a spark of bright.

Guided by moonbeams, softly they gleam,
We trace the outlines of a distant dream.
Paths made of hope, woven in gold,
With every heartbeat, new tales unfold.

Our journey flows like rivers of time,
Each moment precious, a silent rhyme.
With lanterns held high, we chase the dawn,
In illuminated paths, we wander on.

Together we walk, life's gentle dance,
Finding our courage in every chance.
With light by our side, we shall not stray,
On illuminated paths, forever we'll stay.

In the Aura of Morning

The sun peeks through, a gentle glow,
In the aura of morning, the world starts to grow.
Soft breezes whisper, secrets untold,
As nature awakens, its beauty unfolds.

Birds sing sweetly, a melodious tune,
Embraced by the warmth of a waking moon.
Dew on the grass, like jewels on the ground,
In the aura of morning, peace can be found.

Golden rays stretch, painting the sky,
Every color dances as daylight draws nigh.
Moments of magic in silence we find,
In the aura of morning, our hearts are aligned.

Together we breathe in the magic and light,
In the aura of morning, our spirits take flight.
With hope in our hearts and dreams in our sight,
We cherish these moments, so pure and so bright.

Heartbeats in Brilliance

In the quiet night, where dreams ignite,
Heartbeats in brilliance, a shimmering sight.
Stars softly twinkle, guiding our way,
In the stillness of darkness, hope leads the fray.

Waves of emotion, like tides ebb and flow,
Each pulse a reminder of love's gentle glow.
We dance with shadows, in unison sway,
Heartbeats in brilliance, lighting the way.

Moments unfurl like petals in bloom,
Carrying whispers that banish all gloom.
In laughter and tears, our stories entwine,
Heartbeats in brilliance, forever align.

Together we journey, hand in hand tight,
Through valleys of sorrow, to peaks of delight.
With courage and grace, our fears we betray,
In heartbeats of brilliance, love leads the way.

Shadows that Dazzle

In twilight's embrace, shadows begin to play,
Dancing in silence, they twirl and sway.
A tapestry woven in dark and in light,
Shadows that dazzle, a beautiful sight.

Each curve and contour holds secrets untold,
Stories of ages, in whispers unfold.
Mysterious figures that glide ever near,
Shadows that dazzle, ignite ancient fear.

Beneath the soft glow of a waning moon,
The night comes alive with an echoing tune.
In the stillness we wander, lost in the gray,
Shadows that dazzle lead us astray.

Yet in their embrace, we find something dear,
A dance of existence, both fragile and clear.
With every heartbeat, we honor the night,
In shadows that dazzle, we discover our light.

Serenity in Brilliance

In the quiet dawn we rise,
Gentle whispers touch the skies.
Colors dance in soft embrace,
Nature's breath grants us space.

Leaves shimmer in golden light,
Harmony sways, pure delight.
Every moment softly glows,
Serenity in brilliance flows.

Rippling waters sing their song,
Time pauses, nothing feels wrong.
Beneath the clouds, the sun shines bright,
In this realm, all feels right.

Take a breath and hold it near,
In stillness, find what you hold dear.
Each heartbeat sings a tender hymn,
In brilliance found, life's light won't dim.

Shattered Horizons

In the twilight, shadows creep,
Dreams once bright now fall asleep.
Fractured visions haunt the night,
Hope lies heavy in the fight.

Beneath the storms, the echoes stray,
Memories lost, they fade away.
Crimson skies of grief and pain,
Whispers linger, love's disdain.

Fragments glimmer, shards of grace,
In the dark, we seek a trace.
Through the cracks, the light breaks through,
Unraveling the shades of blue.

Yet from ruin, we will rise,
Find the strength behind our sighs.
Shattered horizons can repair,
In the depths, there's hope laid bare.

The Light Between

Between the stars, a silver thread,
Whispers of the dreams we've bred.
Through the silence, we will find,
A gentle truth that soars, unconfined.

In the shadows, secrets weave,
Moments shared that we believe.
In the twilight's soft embrace,
It's the light that fills the space.

Echoes of love, softly spoken,
Promises made that aren't broken.
In the depth of what we seek,
The light between is what we speak.

Together we'll break down the walls,
Find the magic in the calls.
In the stillness, hearts will gleam,
The light between, our shared dream.

A World Aglow

In the dawn, a world aglow,
Dew-kissed petals gently show.
Colors burst, the day awakes,
Nature's song, the heart it shakes.

Golden rays kiss the morning dew,
Whispers echo, fresh and new.
In the light, pure joy ignites,
Bringing warmth to endless heights.

Forests hum with vibrant life,
Peaceful moments, free from strife.
In every heart, a spark will grow,
Together in this world aglow.

Underneath the endless skies,
Laughter dances, never lies.
With each breath, we weave the thread,
A world aglow, where dreams are fed.

Where Luminescence Meets

In twilight's grasp, the colors blend,
Soft whispers of light, they ascend.
Stars begin their gentle dance,
Dreams take flight in a brimming trance.

Beneath the veil of a moonlit sky,
Hope is scattered, shimmering high.
Where shadows fade, new journeys start,
The glow of dusk warms every heart.

Silhouettes of trees, tall and wide,
In their embrace, secrets bide.
Nights alive with a soothing tone,
Where luminescence sings alone.

A canvas rich with hues so rare,
Each moment crafted with gentle care.
Time stands still at this sacred retreat,
Where light and dreams joyfully meet.

Castles of Illumination

In valleys deep, where shadows dwell,
Stand castles bright, their stories tell.
Towers rise to touch the sky,
Illuminated by dreams that fly.

Each stone aglow with a tale of old,
Whispers of warmth, embracing the cold.
Windows gleam like stars aflame,
Guarding secrets, calling their name.

Beyond the walls, the fairies roam,
Dancing light 'round their crystal home.
In every shadow, a flicker, a spark,
Where imagination leaves its mark.

Here, the tales of wonder unfold,
In spaces where the heart turns bold.
Castles gleam under a silver beam,
Illuminated by every dream.

The Golden Hour's Promise

The sun dips low, a tender sigh,
Cascading gold across the sky.
Each ray a promise, warm and bright,
Whispering dreams in fading light.

Fields aglow in honeyed hue,
Nature's brush paints a world anew.
Moments linger, soft and sweet,
In the hush, where all hearts meet.

As shadows stretch, we hold our breath,
Captured time, defying death.
In that hour where magic plays,
Promises echo in gentle waves.

A dance of light, a fleeting glance,
Hope ignites in this golden trance.
The day bids peace, the night draws near,
In the golden hour, we shed our fear.

Flickering Fireflies

In summer's embrace, beneath the trees,
Fireflies dance on the evening breeze.
Tiny stars with a glowing trace,
Mystical lights in a darkened space.

Whispers of laughter fill the air,
Magic tickles without a care.
Each flicker tells of tales untold,
Chasing dreams in the twilight gold.

A fleeting moment, caught in flight,
With every shimmer, dreams ignite.
In the gentle night where quiet sighs,
We chase the glow of the fireflies.

Time drifts softly, wrapped in grace,
Lost in wonder, we find our place.
With hearts aglow, we join the chase,
Where flickering fireflies leave their trace.